Sitting Bull

Roben Alarcon, M.A. Ed.

Table of Contents

Lakota Chief

In the early 1800s, the government began moving American Indians to **reservations** (rez-uhr-VAY-shuhnz). White settlers wanted more land. Most tribes did not give up their land without a fight.

Chief Sitting Bull and the Lakota Indians fought hard. In the end, they could not win. They had to move to reservations. Sitting Bull died still wishing for the Lakota Indians to be free to live where they wished.

▲ This portrait of Sitting Bull was taken after he became a well-known chief.

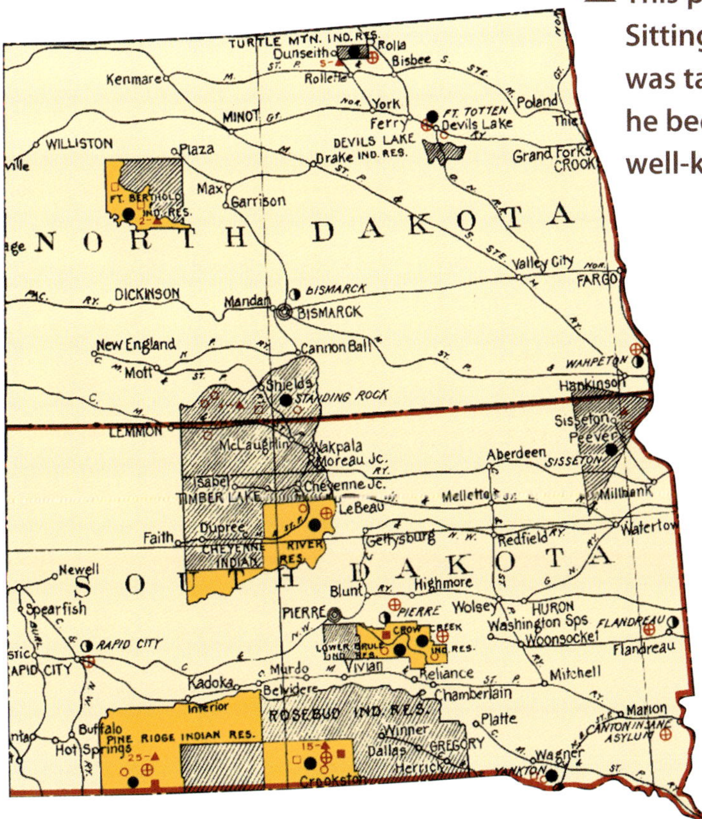

This map of the Dakotas shows the Indian reservations in the region where Sitting Bull lived. Yellow areas are the reservations in the 1920s. Gray areas show how big the reservations used to be. ▶

A Boy with Many Names

Sitting Bull was a Lakota Indian. He grew up in a small **band** called the Hunkpapa. No one knows the year of his birth, or even the place. Sitting Bull believed he was born by the Missouri River around 1831. He could never remember who told him this information, though.

Sitting Bull did not always have this name. At first, he was called Jumping Badger. Later, he was called Slow because he was so careful. He always thought before he acted.

▲ This woodcut shows a Lakota village.

Killing a Bison

Sitting Bull killed his first bison at age ten. Bison are large, strong animals. This was a great achievement for such a young child.

▲ Indians hunting bison on the Plains

▼ When Sitting Bull grew up, he had children of his own and helped give them special names.

Becoming a Warrior

The Lakota were strong **warriors** (WOR-yuhrs). The men gained respect through battle. They used handmade weapons when fighting.

Courage was very important to the Lakota Indians. They did not always try to kill their enemies. Sometimes, a warrior would only sneak up and touch his enemy with a **coup** (KOO) **stick**. They thought that it was braver to do this than to kill the man. It showed great skill to get that close and live.

Changing Names

A Lakota Indian might not keep his or her name from birth. Names were given as an honor. A person's name could be changed if he or she did something smart or bold.

The Coup Stick

Feathers on a coup stick were earned from acts of courage. Each feather showed that the warrior had accomplished something brave.

An Indian warrior holding a coup stick with many feathers.

▲ This is a group of Crow Indians.

The Crow Indians were enemies of the Lakota. Both tribes fought over **sacred** (SAY-kruhd) land. During a fight with the Crow Indians, Slow knocked a man off of his horse. This was Slow's first **coup**. He became a warrior that day. That is when his father gave him the name Sitting Bull.

Supreme Chief of the Lakota

Most American Indian tribes had more than one **chief**. The Cherokee (CHAIR-uh-key) Indians had a war chief and a peace chief. The two chiefs worked together to solve problems with other tribes. The Comanche (kuh-MAN-chee) Indians had three chiefs.

Sitting Bull was the Hunkpapa war chief for years. He worked hard to protect the tribe. His people respected him.

Sitting Bull put on his best clothing for this painted portrait.

▲ These Indians are meeting to work out differences between their tribes.

When white settlers began to enter the Lakota land, the Indians grew angry. All the bands of Lakota Indians had a meeting. They chose Sitting Bull to be their head chief.

Great Honor

The bands of Lakota liked having their own chiefs. They were very independent. There had never been one chief in charge of all the bands. Sitting Bull was the first. The Lakota Indians really looked up to him.

▲ This is a painting that shows Fort Laramie in the Wyoming Territory.

Refusing to Sign

Sitting Bull did not like **treaties**. Treaties were agreements between the tribes and the government. He did not trust the United States government to do what it promised.

The Fort Laramie Treaty of 1868 promised the Lakota Indians a large reservation. Sitting Bull would not sign the treaty. He did not want to give up the Lakota way of life. His tribe had always been free to move where they wanted.

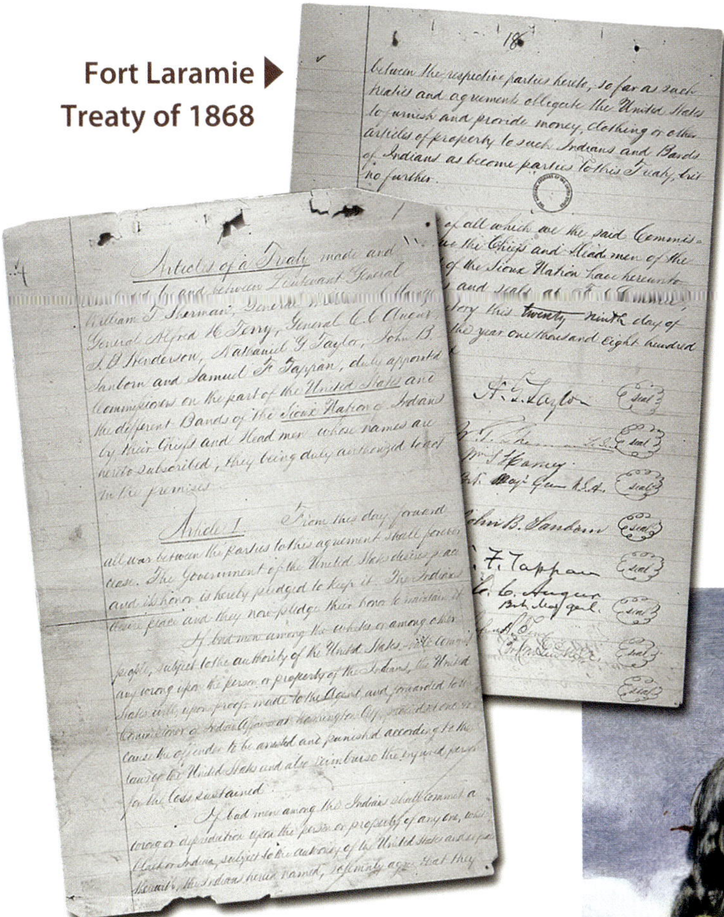

between the respective parties hereto, so far as such treaties and agreements obligate the United States to furnish and provide money, clothing or other articles of property to such Indians and Bands of Indians as become parties to this Treaty, but no further.

In testimony of all which we the said Commissioners and we the Chiefs and Head men of the Sioux Nation have hereunto set our hands and seals at Fort Laramie ... this twenty ninth day of ... the year one thousand eight hundred ...

Articles of a Treaty made and concluded by and between Lieutenant General William T. Sherman, General ... General Alfred H. Terry, General C. C. Augur, J. B. Henderson, Nathaniel G. Taylor, John B. Sanborn and Samuel F. Tappan, duly appointed commissioners on the part of the United States and the different Bands of the Sioux Nation of Indians by their Chiefs and Head men whose names are hereto subscribed, they being duly authorized to act in the premises.

Article 1. From this day forward all war between the parties to this agreement shall forever cease. The Government of the United States desires peace and its honor is hereby pledged to keep it. The Indians desire peace and they now pledge their honor to maintain it.

Fort Laramie Treaty of 1868

Did He Sign?

Sitting Bull said he would never sign a treaty, but his name is on one. The Fort Laramie Treaty has the name "Sitting Bull" on it. Some people think that another chief went to the meeting in Sitting Bull's place. Maybe the other chief signed Sitting Bull's name to the treaty.

Chief Red Cloud signed the treaty. He was from a different band of Lakota. He lost the respect of many people in the tribe when he signed the document. They thought he had given away their freedom.

Chief Red Cloud

▲ This man is looking for gold without permission.

Fighting for the Black Hills

The Black Hills were part of the Lakota land. The Lakota Indians believed that the Black Hills were sacred. They believed that the Lakota Indians had once lived underneath the Black Hills.

One day, white miners found gold in the Black Hills. From that point on, everything changed. Miners came from everywhere. They entered the Black Hills without permission. The Lakota Indians were very angry.

The government tried to buy the Black Hills. The Lakota would not sell the tribal land. Sitting Bull called the Lakota tribes together. He told them that they must fight. The Indians began to attack the white people who came on their land.

The United States Army began moving troops into the area. A famous general named George Custer led his men right into Sitting Bull's warriors. The two sides fought the Battle of Little Bighorn. In this terrible battle, the Lakota and some Cheyenne (shy-AN) Indians outnumbered the army troops. General Custer and all of his men were killed.

General George Custer

Mystical Vision

Before the Battle of Little Bighorn, Sitting Bull danced for many hours without food or water. Then he had a vision. He saw the army soldiers falling like grasshoppers from the sky. He knew then that the Lakota would win the battle ahead.

▼ The Battle of Little Bighorn on June 25, 1876

Moving to Standing Rock

The government was shocked that the army had lost the Battle of Little Bighorn. It sent many troops to force the Lakota tribes to move. One by one, the chiefs surrendered. Many bands of Lakota were moved to reservations.

Sitting Bull and William Cody

Wild West Show

A man named William "Buffalo Bill" Cody started the Wild West Show. Everyone was surprised when Sitting Bull said he would join the show. Chief Sitting Bull was paid $50 a week to ride a horse.

Sitting Bull took his people into Canada. They headed north to save their freedom. It was hard to live in Canada. There were few bison to hunt. The tribe almost starved. Sitting Bull finally had to bring his people back and surrender.

The government sent Sitting Bull to jail for two years. Then, he joined his band at the Standing Rock Reservation in the Dakota Territory (TAIR-uh-tor-ee).

Annie Oakley

Nickname from Sitting Bull

Another person in the Wild West Show was Annie Oakley. Oakley was famous for her shooting skills. Sitting Bull gave her the nickname "Little Sure Shot."

▲ These Lakota Indians are performing the Ghost Dance.

Ghost Dance

In 1890, an Indian dance called the Ghost Dance became popular. The Indians missed the way things used to be. When they danced, they felt closer to their old way of life. Many Lakota Indians began doing the dance on their reservations.

The government started to get nervous. The dance was very fast and energetic. It seemed like the dance might make the Indians want to fight. The white men wanted to keep the Indians under control.

Government leaders wanted to talk to Sitting Bull. They knew he was a strong chief. They thought he might be pushing the tribes to do the Ghost Dance.

Indian policemen went to Standing Rock Reservation. They arrested Sitting Bull. His friends did not want to let him go. A fight broke out and guns were fired. Sitting Bull was accidentally shot and killed by two Lakota police officers.

▼ The fight during the capture of Sitting Bull

▲ Lakota police officers Red Tomahawk and Eagle Man. Red Tomahawk was the man who killed Sitting Bull.

Buried in two places?

There is an argument over where Sitting Bull is buried today. He was first buried in North Dakota. Then some of his tribe stole his bones and buried them in South Dakota. Some say the bones they took were not Sitting Bull's. No one knows for sure where the bones truly are.

Other Indian Chiefs

Sitting Bull was not the only brave Indian chief to resist the move to reservations. The stories of two other brave chiefs follow.

Chief Little John of the Cherokee

John Ross was chosen as chief of the Cherokee tribe in 1828. He was only one-eighth Cherokee. But, he was still admired by many tribal members.

Soon after Ross became chief, the Indian Removal Act was passed. This law allowed the government to move tribes out of the East. The government now had the power to force the tribes to move onto reservations in the West.

John Ross

Trail of Tears

Little John's wife died along the Trail of Tears. She gave her only blanket to a sick child. Her thin clothing could not protect her in such terrible weather, and she died.

The removal of the Cherokee to the West in 1838

One small band of Cherokee signed a treaty with the government. This treaty stated that the tribe would move peacefully. However, the rest of the Cherokee Indians were against the treaty. Chief John Ross tried to explain the mistake to the government workers. The government made the treaty **official** (uh-FISH-uhl) anyway.

The tribe was given two years to move. Since members of the tribe did not agree with the treaty, they stayed on their land. The army came and forced the Cherokee to move west. The Cherokee had to walk thousands of miles. Many of them died along the way. The terrible walk was called the Trail of Tears.

Other Indian Chiefs *(cont.)*

Chief Joseph of the Nez Percé

Chief Joseph was a leader of the Nez Percé tribe. The Nez Percé lived on a large reservation in the Northwest. Then, white miners found gold on their land. The government wanted to make the reservation smaller. This way, land could be given to miners and settlers.

Chief Joseph would not sign a new treaty with the government. He met with government leaders. He was hoping they would change their minds. They never did. He did not change his mind either.

One day, some Nez Percé warriors attacked white settlers. The United States Army came to force the tribe to a smaller reservation. A long battle began. It did not end for three months. Chief Joseph and his people grew tired of fighting. But, they were very proud and did not want to give up. Finally, they knew they had no choice. Chief Joseph had to **surrender** (suh-REN-duhr) to the army.

Chief Joseph

▲ Fighting between the Nez Percé and the United States Army

Fight No More Forever

When he surrendered, Chief Joseph made a speech that has become famous. At the end of his speech, he said, "Hear me, my chiefs! I am tired. My heart is sick and sad. From where the sun now stands, I will fight no more forever."

This shows Chief Joseph ▶ after his surrender to the army.

Life on the Reservation

American Indians fought for years to stay out of the reservations. However, the United States government was too powerful. The Indian tribes were forced to change.

At first, Indian reservations were just areas of land saved for tribes. The Indians could still live as they pleased. Later, reservations were like small cities. **Agents** were hired to be in charge. These agents passed out food and supplies sent by the government.

Reservations were used to teach the Indians how to live like white settlers. The Indian children went to school. The adults also learned new skills. They were taught to farm, sew, and bake.

▲ Pine Ridge Reservation in 1891

Reservations Today

Today, Indian reservations still exist. They are like small countries. The members of the tribe choose people to be in charge. Then, these leaders make rules for everyone on the tribal land to follow.

▼ This is the Indian School on the Pine Ridge Reservation in South Dakota.

▼ Teachers and employees of a reservation school

The 1800s were a difficult time for the American Indians. Sitting Bull and other brave Indians helped their people fight to save their ways of life. The tribes believed that no one owned the land. People should share and respect the land's resources. To the very end of his life, Sitting Bull worked to help his people succeed.

Glossary

agents—people sent by the government to work on the reservations

band—small part of a larger tribe who live and work together

chief—leader of an Indian tribe

coup—courageous act

coup stick—symbol held by Indian warriors to show their bravery

official—formal; legal

reservations—lands set aside especially for Indians to live and work

sacred—holy or worthy of respect

surrender—give up power or control

treaties—agreements or contracts between groups

vision—dream that tells of the future; it can happen when you are awake or asleep

warriors—young, brave Indian men who fought to protect their tribes